This book may be k...

AN ALBUM OF AUTOMOBILE RACING

AN ALBUM OF

Automobile Racing

BY W. E. BUTTERWORTH

FRANKLIN WATTS | NEW YORK | LONDON | 1977

Cover design by Nick Krenitsky

Photographs courtesy of:

Brown Brothers: pp. 9, 10, 11, 13; Daytona International Speedway: pp. 88 (all), 91 (top left, center); Indianapolis Motor Speedway: pp. 39 (top & bottom), 41, 42 (top), 57, 58, 61 (bottom), 91 (left center), 93; N.A.S.C.A.R.: pp. 80, 83, 84, 85, 86 (top & bottom), 87, 90, 91 (right top, center, bottom & left bottom); National Automotive History Collection, Detroit Public Library: pp. 14, 17, 19, 20, 21, 25, 26, 29, 31, 32, 33, 35, 37 (top & bottom), 40, 42 (bottom), 43, 44, 45, 46, 48, 49 (top & bottom), 50 (top & bottom), 53, 54, 56, 60, 61 (top), 63, 78 (top & bottom), 79; Oldsmobile: pp. 18, 22; United Press International: pp. 64, 65, 66, 68, 69, 70 (top & bottom), 71, 72, 73, 74 (top & bottom), 76, 77, 92; W.H.G. France, Sr.: p. 82.

Library of Congress Cataloging in Publication Data

Butterworth, William E
    An album of automobile racing.

    Bibliography: p.
    Includes index.
    SUMMARY: Discusses the history of automobile racing concentrating on early twentieth-century races and the development of faster cars.
    1. Automobile racing—History—Juvenile Literature. [1. Automobile racing—History. 2. Automobiles—History] I. Title.
GV1029.5.B87   796.7′2′09   77–6363
ISBN 0–531–02909–3

CONTENTS

AN ALBUM OF AUTOMOBILE RACING

AUTOMOBILES: AN OLD IDEA

In Homer's *Iliad*, which goes back at least seven hundred years before the birth of Christ, there is a reference to tricycles: According to Homer, Vulcan in a single day made twenty of them, which,

(Wondrous to tell) instinct with spirit roll'd
From place to place around the blest abodes,
Self-moved, obedient to the beck of gods.

While some people might smile at the mental picture of twenty gods and goddesses merrily rolling around the "blest abodes" on tricycles, like so many first graders at recess, it was really the science fiction of its time. Here was a *machine* to carry people from here to there faster than they could walk or run, and which did not, like the horse, donkey, or elephant, have to be trained, fed, or cared for.

And it's not at all hard to imagine that the first automobile race of all time took place right there, in the "blest abodes," when two tricycle-mounted gods decided to find out who had the fastest tricycle.

THE FIRST POWERED VEHICLES

Two thousand years passed before anyone came up with the idea of a powered personal vehicle. Leonardo da Vinci, who some call the greatest genius of all time, is known to have thought about an automobile (the word simply means a self-propelled vehicle) but apparently the problems of making one work were too much even for him.

In 1740, Jacques de Vaucanson rolled down a Paris street in what many people think was the first self-powered vehicle. If it were possible to make a clock work by means of wound springs and gears, he had reasoned, there was no reason that you couldn't make a carriage move the same way. All that he needed was a very large clock motor. He built one, wound it up, and it did indeed propel a horseless carriage down the street, but not very far.

Twenty years later, a Swiss clergyman, J. H. Genevois, improved on de Vaucanson's idea by putting windmills on his horseless carriage. The idea was that the windmills would wind the clock motor, and then the clock motor would propel the carriage. It worked, but not very well.

In 1769 Captain Nicholas Joseph Cugnot, of the French artillery, came up with the first really self-propelled vehicle. He thought of it not as an automobile, but rather as a means of moving heavy cannons around on the battlefield. He invented and built a machine that applied the power of a steam engine to the front wheel of a huge tricycle. On its first trial, it moved at about 2.25 mph (3.62 kph) for twenty minutes, carrying four people.

Cugnot's vehicle can be seen today in the Conservatoire des Arts et Métiers in Paris.

The Cugnot steam-driven carriage

THE FIRST AUTOMOBILES

What was needed for an automobile was a power plant, an engine, which would be both light enough and powerful enough to propel the vehicle on which it was mounted. Two Germans, Carl Benz and Gottlieb Daimler, who had experience with internal combustion engines they had originally designed to provide power to factory machine tools, were the first to put their engines to work on vehicles.

The first Benz ran in 1885, and the first Daimler in 1886. Later, the firms founded by the two men merged to become Daimler-

**An 1886 Daimler with
Daimler in it**

The 1887 Benz with Benz in it

Benz, which prospers today. In their lifetimes, however, the two men never met.

In 1896 a man named Emile Jellinek went to the Daimler factory and bought a new Daimler, with the announced intention of reselling it at a profit. In the next year, he bought and resold

140 Daimler automobiles. Every business needs a good salesman, and Jellinek, an Austro-Hungarian businessman, was soon appointed distributor for all Daimler-Benzes sold outside of Germany.

In 1900, possibly because he sensed there was a good deal of anti-German feeling in France, his largest potential market, he decided he needed a new name for the cars. What was needed was a name with a certain style and class . . . and one that didn't sound so German. He announced that henceforth the cars would be called Mercedes, after his daughter.

THE FIRST RACES

Most of the automobiles built before the turn of the century were French. While England was then the most highly industrialized nation on earth, the English government was afraid of automobiles. From 1865 until 1878, any self-propelled vehicle on the road had to be preceded by a person on foot carrying a red flag. The maximum speed was set at 4 mph (6.44 kph). It wasn't until 1894 that the speed limit was *raised* to 14 mph (22.53 kph), and it wasn't until 1904 that the limit went up to 20 mph (32.18 kph).

The United States around 1900 was nothing like the industrial giant it shortly became. In 1903, for example, there were 53,000 automobiles in the entire world, and 30,200 of them had been built in France while most of the rest were German or Italian. Only a few thousand cars had been built in America.

The very first "races" were actually more competition between two cars to see which car could be coaxed into running longest before it broke down. There was a "trial" between automobiles in 1894, running from Paris to Rouen, and the next year saw the first real race: A Panhard-Levassor automobile zoomed from Paris to Bordeaux in the remarkable time of only forty-eight hours, and at the sizzling speed of 15 mph (24.14 kph).

THE FIRST AMERICAN AUTO MANUFACTURER

Most of the first cars in America were imported from Europe. The Steinway Piano Company, for example, became the American dealer for Daimler cars in 1891. The first "horseless carriage" was exactly that: a horse carriage to which an engine had been attached. The first in America to build one were the Duryea Brothers (Charles E. and J. Frank) in 1892–93. It first ran on September 21, 1893. Three years later Henry Ford built his first car.

**The Duryea
horseless carriage**

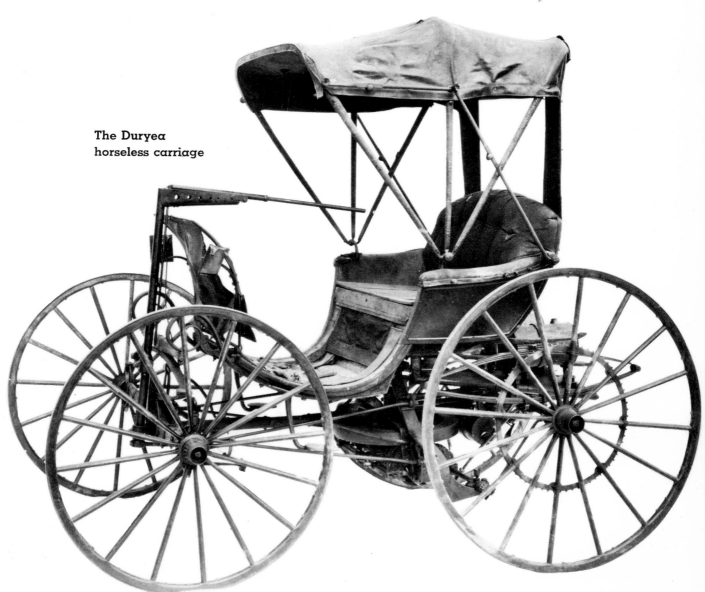

THE FIRST AMERICAN AUTO RACES

The first "official" auto race in America was in Chicago, where the *Chicago Times-Herald* newspaper, primarily to build its circulation, sponsored a race in Jackson Park in 1895.

A year later, in the summer of 1896, the first auto race on a race track was held at Narragansett Park in Providence, Rhode Island.

Most of early American competition was designed to show off the ruggedness and reliability of the machine, rather than car against car. "Trials" were held for endurance and distance and also to see how steep a hill could be climbed.

THE GORDON BENNETT TROPHY RACES

European and especially French domination of auto racing disturbed James Gordon Bennett, Jr., publisher of the *New York Herald.* Bennett was one of the first, and certainly one of the most vocal, prominent Americans to understand that the United States was on the doorstep of becoming the most powerful nation in the world.

Just before the first race on a race track started, the summer of 1896 at Narragansett Park, Providence, Rhode Island.

There was no question in Bennett's mind that the United States would quickly become the world leader in anything to do with automobiles just as soon as the American people came to think of the automobile as something American. If an American car, he reasoned, could win an international auto race, the imagination of the American people would be caught, and American ingenuity would go on from there.

In 1899 Bennett went to the French Automobile Club and offered not only to help pay the expenses of a series of international races, but to contribute the trophy to be given to the winner. It was quite a trophy. Constructed of marble, gold, and silver, there was a model of the last word in fast automobiles. A young man stood on the hood, holding a flaming torch in one upraised hand. Standing up in the back seat of the car was a woman with wings wearing a flowing gown. Bennett never replied to questions concerning the identity of this odd couple although questions were often raised.

The trophy immediately became something every country wanted for its own, however, and after some bickering, rules for the International Trophy Race, as it was officially called, were decided upon.

The race would cover 500 kilometers (about 312 miles) with the first to be held in France. The country that won the race would serve as host country for the next race. Every part in every car had to be manufactured in the country that entered the car, and each country was permitted three entries. They didn't have to be the same kind of car although they could be.

These were the rules Bennett hoped would see America jump into racing. He thought that at first, we would probably enter three different cars, and then eventually realize that one was best. Then we would enter three identical cars, and greatly increase our chances of winning.

The first race was held in France, between Paris and Lyon. Only five cars competed: three French, a Belgian, and an American. The Belgian named "Red Devil" Jenatzy, roared away from the starting line and promptly got lost. The American entry broke down. A Frenchman named Charron, driving a 20-horsepower Panhard, managed to limp over the finish line, averaging 38.6 mph (62.11 kph) for the distance, and earned himself a place in the record books as the winner of the very first Grand Prix race.

The Gordon Bennett Trophy Races lasted only six years. The French, who felt the rules worked against them, are generally credited with sabotaging the whole idea, or at least easing the Americans out of Grand Prix racing.

THE VANDERBILT RACES

Another American entered the picture in 1904. He decided Bennett's idea had been good, but that it had failed in the execution, probably because Bennett hadn't enough money. There were very few men who could make an observation like this, but William K. Vanderbilt Jr., then the world's richest man, certainly could.

The Vanderbilt Races, he announced, would be far superior to anything ever held in France. He would personally supervise everything.

The first Vanderbilt race, 283 miles (455 km) in distance, was held on October 8, 1904, over a 30-mile (48.27-km) course in Nassau County, Long Island, New York. The authorities were very obliging about roping off the public roads for Mr. Vanderbilt's race, possibly because he and his family owned most of Nassau County.

Mr. Vanderbilt's personal jeweler came up with the trophy (which is now in the Smithsonian Institution). It was made of sterling silver lined with gold, and weighed 40 lbs (18.14 kg). Newspapers in which Mr. Vanderbilt had an interest had printed stories calculated to bring the crowds out. And the crowds came. Three hundred thousand people witnessed that first race. No race since, not even at places like Indianapolis or Daytona Beach, has attracted that many fans.

William K. Vanderbilt at the wheel of
his specially built Vanderbilt Special.
This photograph was taken in the winter
of 1906 at Daytona Beach, Florida. The name
of Vanderbilt's riding mechanic has been lost.

There were nineteen entries: six American (including a
Packard); five German (all Mercedes); two Italian (Fiats); six
French (a Renault, a De Deutrich, a Clement-Bayard and three
Panhards).

A Panhard won, but the driver was an American, George
Heath, which annoyed the French and pleased the Americans.

OTHER EARLY AMERICAN RACING

The automobile bug had bitten America. Manufacturers sprang
up in barns and warehouses all over America. One of these was
a young man named Ransom E. Olds, whose name and initials
live on in the Oldsmobile and Reo trucks.

The 1903 Oldsmobile Pirate, the
first car to break "a mile a minute."
Driver Don Wurgis leans low over the
engine. The tube-like tanks on either
side of the engine were for fuel and water.

In 1903, Olds built the first American car to beat "a mile a
minute," and it set a record of 5 miles (8.05 km) in 6.5 minutes
over the sands at Daytona Beach.

Other "automobilists" were more interested in seeing how
much torture a car would take, than in seeing either how fast it
would go, or whether or not it was faster than someone else's car.
The greatest challenge of all was naturally a cross-country run.
At the time, if all the paved roads in America had been laid end
to end, they would have stretched no farther than between Boston
and New York.

In early 1903, a young physician, H. Nelson Jackson, of Bur-
lington, Vermont, while visiting in San Francisco, accepted what
appeared to be an idle bet. He put up fifty dollars that an automobile could indeed drive from one coast to the other. Then he

went to some pains to win the bet. He bought a new Winton, hired Sewell K. Crocker of Tacoma, Washington, as a chauffeur/mechanic, and started out from the Golden Gate for New York City on May 23. Sixty-three days later, having followed old stage-coach routes and military trails, he arrived in New York on July 26, 1903.

The advertising value of such travel appealed to the Packard Motor Company. Just as soon as they could get a car ready, they dispatched Tom Fetch to cross the country in both directions, alone. Fetch made it from San Francisco to New York in fifty-three days. Fetch had barely finished his run when people began to talk of racing one car against another across the country.

On the way back: Tom Fetch pauses on "Old Pacific," his 1903 Packard, to light his pipe on the return trip to the West Coast.

Laurent Grosso whips around New York's Empire City
Race Course in 1903. His "riding mechanic" hangs
far outboard of the Mercedes to "keep the car from
turning over." How effective this was is open to
debate, but it certainly pleased the paying customers.

So autos moved onto horse tracks, generally to the fury of
horse lovers and the delight of track owners, who had learned
that people would pay hard cash money to watch racing. Some
cynics said that people didn't go to the races to watch the cars,
but to watch the wrecks, and that argument goes on today.

THE FIRST TRANSCONTINENTAL RACE

There were 60,000 registered motor cars in the United States in 1905, and outside of big cities, practically no paved roads. Something had to be done about that, of course, and the National Good Roads Association was formed. When they were trying to call attention to their convention, scheduled for June 1905 in Portland, Oregon, the Good Roads people remembered the talk about a transcontinental race, and decided to hold one.

When asked to provide cars for the race, however, manufacturers were somewhat less than enthusiastic. James W. Abbott, of the U.S. Office of Public Roads, was able to talk only Ransom E. Olds into providing two cars, drivers and mechanics and the necessary funds. The other manufacturers felt that Olds was a fool. The odds against both cars making it across country in one piece were astronomical; it was hard enough, as the Packard had shown, to get across the continent at all. Racing would see the cars reduced to wrecks long before the distance was covered.

Olds felt differently. He had confidence in his cars and believed that the name Oldsmobile would be on everybody's lips as the nation followed the progress of the race in their newspapers.

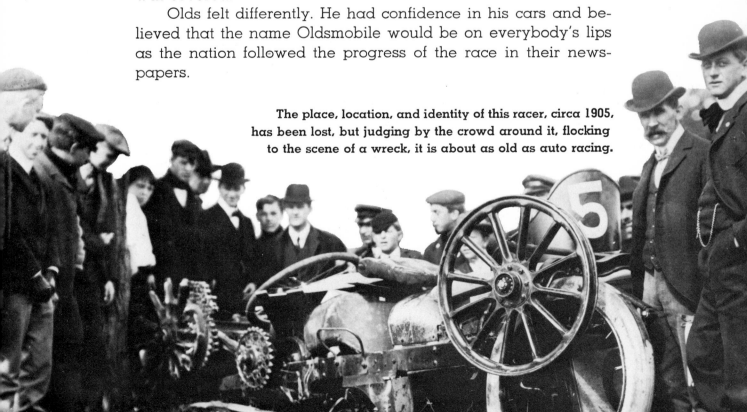

The place, location, and identity of this racer, circa 1905, has been lost, but judging by the crowd around it, flocking to the scene of a wreck, it is about as old as auto racing.

At 9:30 in the morning of May 8, 1905, two "Curved Dash" Oldsmobiles, "Old Scout" (Dwight Huss, driver; Milford Wigle, assistant) and "Old Steady" (Percy F. Megargel, driver; Barton Stanchfield, assistant) took off on the race. The starting point was the Harrold's Oldsmobile-Pierce Arrow dealership on New York City's Columbus Circle.

A week later, the two cars arrived in Chicago. Except for some hub-deep mud in Ohio, the trip was uneventful. From Chicago onward, however, the trip got rougher. It took another thirty-seven days for "Old Scout" to cross the rest of the country, and four more days for "Old Steady" to complete the trip. Their average speed (they drove only in daylight hours) was about 7 mph (11.26 kph) for the trip of 3,890 miles (6,260 km), but the important thing was they had made the trip without complete breakdown.

"Old Steady" and "Old Scout" as they set off from Columbus Circle in New York City on the first Transcontinental Auto Race, May 8, 1905. Note the horns, mounted on the steering tillers, and that "Old Steady" has smaller wheels than "Old Scout." "Old Scout" has its searchlight mounted beside the assistant driver while "Old Steady" has it mounted on the dashboard.

HENRY FORD: RACE DRIVER
AND RACE CAR OWNER

When Henry Ford built his first automobile in 1896, he was chief engineer of the Edison Illuminating Company of Detroit, Michigan (now the Detroit Edison Company). This was quite a position of responsibility for a young man, with generous pay (a hundred dollars a month) to show the company's appreciation. His superiors were rather shocked that an otherwise levelheaded engineer would waste his time on something as frivolous as horseless carriages and told him so.

The disapproval of management grew just about as fast as Henry Ford's belief that there was money to be made with the horseless carriage, it was just a matter of deciding how to make it. In the summer of 1899 it came to the attention of Edison Illuminating Company officials that their chief engineer was moonlighting as production superintendent of the Detroit Automobile Company, and that he even held a small block of stock in the company.

He was summoned to the executive office and informed that, because of their faith in his ability and on account of his loyal service, he was to be promoted to the position of general superintendent of the entire company, with an appropriate raise in pay. There was only one small condition: He would have to stop fooling around with horseless carriages, and devote himself entirely to his new duties. The date was August 15, 1899, and the company records for that day carry the simple notation: "Henry Ford, chief engineer, resigned."

The Detroit Automobile Company was something of a disappointment to Henry Ford. It worked more like a building contractor than a factory. In other words, salespeople went out and sold a car and then returned to the factory with the details. Then the car was built, one part at a time, one car at a time. When the company went out of business in a year, Ford was obviously pleased. He'd make his own cars, his own way.

23—

The way to interest potential customers in Ford cars, he reasoned, was to show how fast they would go. He built a Ford Racer, a two-cylinder machine developing a respectable twenty-six horsepower, and, as soon as he got it running, challenged Alexander Winton to a race.

Winton was the owner and builder of a huge machine that had already dazzled the public by driving over a measured mile in 1 minute, 14.5 seconds, or 48.332 mph (77.77 kph). He immediately accepted Ford's challenge, and the race was set for October 7, 1901, at the Grosse Pointe (Michigan) Race Track. It would be a ten-mile (16.09-km) race.

Ford was left behind at the starting line, as the faster and more powerful Winton raced ahead. However, apparently Winton then made the mistake of trying to humiliate Ford and his car badly, by running his own car as fast as he could. The inevitable happened. The Winton broke down. First it slowed, and Ford passed, and then the Winton collapsed.

It was Ford's turn to humiliate Winton, but he was too smart to do this.

"Mr. Winton is obviously a better racer than I am," he announced graciously. "If he had been driving the Ford, he would have won."

Ford was, after all, selling cars, not his services as a race driver.

Once the word had gotten around that Ford had built a car that had beat the mighty Winton, he was again able to come up with money to start another automobile company. This one was named The Henry Ford Company, for the backers wanted to take advantage of the publicity he had earned by beating Winton.

Ford, meanwhile, had changed his mind. Instead of building a large number of cars, at as cheap a price as possible, he wanted to make really special cars, selling them on the reputation he had, and would continue to make, on the race course.

The board of directors of the company found they could not reason with Ford, so they brought in somebody who, they thought, could handle him. This was Henry M. Leland, of Faulconer & Leland, the largest—and best—machine shop in the United States.

Mr. Leland got no further with Ford than anybody else had, and it was mutually decided that Henry Ford would have to leave the Henry Ford Company. As part of his price for getting out, Ford insisted that the Henry Ford Company could not call any of its cars "Fords." Leland and his board of directors finally gave in. The Henry Ford Company would no longer make Fords. They would make and sell cars under the name of a French explorer who had been in the Detroit area: Cadillac.

Henry Ford immediately set to work building a car that would be the unquestioned ruler of the race track. It was an enormous machine. The wheelbase was 117 inches (297.18 cm), and the tread (the distance between the wheels) was 5 feet 6 inches (167.64 cm). It had four pistons with 7-inch (17.78-cm) diameters, moving through a 7-inch stroke; this is what is known as a "square engine." It developed 70 horsepower and was so large and heavy that Henry Ford, a practical man, took a final look at it and decided that it needed a professional driver. A man named Barney Oldfield, who had been a professional bicycle racer, was hired to drive the car, which Ford christened the "Ford 999."

Henry Ford stands beside the 999. Barney Oldfield, a former professional bicycle racer who became one of the most famous of auto racers, holds the two-handled steering tiller.

Alexander Winton tested his
Bullet on the hard packed white
sands of Daytona Beach in 1904.

Winton, who had been anxious for a rematch after his defeat, agreed to run against the 999 in October 1902, again at Grosse Pointe. Other cars were entered, other builders having seen the commercial value of winning, but the race was really between Winton and his Winton and Oldfield in Ford's 999. It was really no contest; the 999 was a vastly superior automobile.

The prestige Ford earned with the 999 was enough to get him enough money to start another automobile company. This one he called the Ford Motor Company, and this one he controlled. It went into business in 1903 about six months after the 999's Grosse Pointe victory.

But while he devoted most of his time to managing the affairs of his new company, Ford also wondered whether he had been right about turning over the steering tiller to a professional. After all, *he* had defeated Winton first. He built another racer, the Model K, and in August 1905, attempted to set a world speed record. He didn't make it and never raced publicly again.

RACING ON THE FLORIDA SAND

In 1870 an Ohio Yankee named Mathias Day journeyed to the then nearly tropical wilderness of Florida and became very impressed with the land where the Halifax River meets the Atlantic Ocean, 90 miles (145 km) southeast of Jacksonville. He laid out the plans for a city, and in 1876, the city was named for him: Daytona.

Until the automobile came along, the area served primarily as a resort for well-to-do Northerners and a haven for those without any money who scrounged a living as best they could in the warm sunshine.

On both sides of the mouth of the Halifax River (which is really more of a tidal lagoon) there are broad beaches, about 500 feet (152.40 m) wide at low tide. The consistency of the sand is such that when the waters recede, the sand is both quite flat and very densely packed. It makes, in other words, a fine place to race cars. South of the mouth of the river is New Smyrna, which has a fine beach on which races were held, but north of the mouth, on Daytona and Ormond Beaches, the sand stretches for 23 miles (37 km), and for more than half a century, the beaches served as the world's fastest race course.

THE STANLEY STEAMER: THE FASTEST CAR IN THE WORLD

Twin brothers F. E. and F. O. Stanley, identical down to the way they trimmed their full beards and mustaches, were convinced the future of the automobile lay not with a noisy, dirty, internal combustion gasoline engine but with quiet, clean, steam power.

They pointed out that railroads had been around a long time, and a good deal was known about steam: all it would require was to adapt what was already known about steam locomotives for use on steam automobiles.

Then they went out and built their own steam automobile, officially known as the Stanley Steam Car but called the "Stanley Steamer" by everybody but the Stanley Brothers.

Auto racers, Ford, Oldfield and Winton among them, treated the brothers with barely concealed scorn. At least until the Stanley Brothers took one of their cars to the white sands at Daytona.

Sir Thomas Dewar, a wealthy Englishman, had come up with "The Dewar Cup" and a cash prize to the car that could cross a measured mile in the shortest time. Cars came from all over the world to the tests, held in January 1905.

Much to the chagrin of Ford, Oldfield, Winton and others, one of the funny looking little Stanley Steamers, with Louis Ross driving, won the race hands down, passing over the measured mile (1.609 km) in 38 seconds. That was 94.736 mph (152.43 kph), far faster than Ford, Oldfield, Winton, and company thought possible.

People don't like to believe what they don't want to believe, so there was much public skepticism about how fast the Stanley Steamer had *really* gone. The Stanley Brothers returned the next year, with an improved version of their car.

During the week January 21–28, 1906, they set the following world's records, with Fred Marriott driving:

DISTANCE	TIME	NEW RECORD	OLD RECORD
1 kilometer:	18.4 seconds	195.65 kilometers per hour	168.22 kph
1 mile:	28.2 seconds	127.65 miles per hour	104.65 mph
1 mile in competition:	31.2 seconds	115.38 miles per hour	86.95 mph
5 miles:	2 minutes, 47.2 seconds	107.46 miles per hour	91.37 mph
2 miles:	59.6 seconds	120.80 miles per hour	————

When these records were set, there were ten times as many unofficial timers as there were official timers, so there was no question whatever that the Stanley Steamer had puffed and wheezed its way to victory over the mighty gas engine cars.

The Stanley Steam Car Racer returned the next year, again with Fred Marriott at the wheel. Marriott made a trial run over the measured mile, crossing it in 29.5 seconds (122.03 mph or 196.35 kph), and then decided to go for a record.

He went back up the beach nine miles (14 km) to get up speed before he crossed the starting line. The engine was adjusted to generate 1300 lbs (589.67 kg) per square inch of steam pressure to the wheels, where before only 800–1,000 lbs (362–453 kg) had been used.

Fred Marriott flashes past the starting timer at Daytona Beach in 1907. Less than a minute later, he encountered uneven sand and wrecked the car. When this picture was taken, he was traveling well over 150 mph (241.35 kph) and was the fastest man in the fastest car in the world.

About one-quarter of the way through the mile, the Steamer hit a rough patch of sand. The car flipped, and flew more than a hundred feet through the air before landing again at an angle and destroying itself. Marriott was unconscious when they reached him, and one eye was hanging out of its socket. One Dr. Parks, a Boston physician who was among the first to reach him, put the eye back where it belonged. Marriott quickly recovered his full health, but the Stanley Steamers never raced again.

"The most valuable lesson learned by this accident," the brothers said in a joint statement, "was the great danger such terrific speed incurs. So we have decided never again to risk the life of a courageous man for such a small return."

By computing the distance and time from the starting line to the place where the Stanley Steamer left the ground, they were able to determine that Marriott was going 177.27 mph (285.23 kph) when he lost control of the car.

Seventy years later, 177.27 mph is considered very good speed indeed at the Daytona International Raceway.

J. WALTER CHRISTIE: RACE DRIVING GENIUS

One of the most famous race drivers and race car builders of the early years was J. Walter Christie. However, unlike others of his mechanical genius (Ford, Edison, Westinghouse, and the like) Christie is just about forgotten today.

When the very first submarine in the U.S. Navy sank at its moorings at the Brooklyn Navy Yard, it was brought to the surface and salvaged by J. Walter Christie, who was then twenty-one years old.

With that behind him, Christie turned his inventive genius to naval cannons. Smokeless powder, which created far greater pressures than the old black powder had, caused great problems in recoil for naval cannons. Christie came up with a means to

J. Walter Christie at the wheel of one
of his cars, about to make a speed trial
at Ormond (Daytona) Beach in 1905.

absorb this great force, and made possible the long-range naval
cannons used by all navies in the world to this day.

He participated in auto racing, both as a driver and as a
designer and builder of cars, and was as well known in his era
as Barney Oldfield, Henry Ford, Alex Winton, or Eddie Rickenbacker had been in theirs.

Even before World War I came Christie was convinced that
the U.S. Army would need military type automobiles and trac-
tors, and started to build them before most people thought the
U.S. would ever be involved. His trackdrawn artillery mover was
thirty years ahead of its time, and the U.S. Army never bought it.

In the 1920s he invented a tank suspension system, and built
a tank that would go 70 mph (112.63 kph) on the ground, and
could "swim" rivers. He demonstrated this vehicle by swimming
the Hudson River from New Jersey to New York City and then
racing down Fifth Avenue at 70 mph. The U.S. Army, whose
tanks could go about 8 mph (12.87 kph) and could not swim, was
not at all interested.

The Russians were. They bought Christie's patents, and the
vast majority of Soviet tanks of World War II and even today use
Christie's suspension system. Broke and embittered, Christie died
in the early days of World War II.

FASTER AND FASTER;
FARTHER AND FARTHER

About 1905–06, the tiller gave way entirely to the steering wheel. Engineers succeeded in building engines that were more powerful, less heavy, and more reliable. The radiator (the word comes from "radiation," radiating heat away from the engine) was moved out in front, where it remained. Better wheels were developed.

The major problem facing racing drivers and ordinary motorists as well was tires. Auto tires of the day were nothing more than enlarged versions of bicycle tires. Cloth (most often cotton) was impregnated with rubber, and several layers were formed into a tire. As the tire flexed (and the higher the speed, the more it flexed) the cloth fibers rubbed against each other, generated heat, and either melted the rubber or broke, or both.

Barney Oldfield poses for a publicity photograph at the wheel of a Peerless "Green Dragon" racer in 1907. Judging from the board roadway and the ropes connected to the frame of the Green Dragon and the car behind, the photo was taken as the car was being moved, over an open roof, from one part of the Peerless assembly line to another.

Prepared to race around the world, the crew of the
Thomas "Flyer" posed proudly, with flag flying,
before the start of the 1908 New York to Paris Race.

Automobile competition was still divided into two major categories: speed, which meant that because of the tires, races were
over either a measured mile, or several miles; or endurance,
which meant races were over great distances, or through rough
terrain.

About the longest race of the endurance type was the New
York to Paris Race of 1908. The course was overland from New
York to the West Coast, by ship to Siberia, and across Russia (by
what roads there were, but generally by rail) to Western Europe.

The American entry, the Thomas "Flyer," won, and once this honor had been won, Americans seemed to lose interest in foreign racing.

Speed, rather than endurance, was obviously what fired the American imagination.

ELECTRIC CARS

The idea of powering cars by the use of electricity fascinated some people. In 1903 Walter C. Baker, who had founded the Baker Motor Vehicle Company, which manufactured electric-powered trucks, designed and built an electric racer, the "Baker Torpedo." It had a $5/8$-hp motor, which drew its power from twelve storage batteries. It ran well, more than a mile (1.609 km) in a minute, but when the mile was over, so was the power.

THE BOARD TRACKS

As racing became a business, it had to face the problem of what to do with a dirt track in the rain. Horses could run in the mud; cars could not. Wood was then plentiful and cheap, and the obvious solution. Board tracks were laid, with just enough space between the planks to let the rain drain through.

A Mercedes Benz, circa 1914, on a board track (probably the Empire State Raceway). The driver is Tommy Milton (left). Note the crank, neatly tied out of the way with leather strap. The round object atop the radiator is a water temperature gauge.

THE INDIANAPOLIS MOTOR SPEEDWAY

In 1908 four Indianapolis businessmen, Carl G. Fisher, James A. Allison, Arthur C. Newby and Frank H. Wheeler, pooled their money and began to build what they thought of as a "great outdoor laboratory" for automobiles. It was intended to provide a place where automobile and auto parts manufacturers (Fisher and Allison among them) could test their products safely, under controlled conditions; it also featured a track designed specifically for auto racing.

They acquired a parcel of property in Indianapolis a mile (1.609 km) long and half a mile (.8 km) wide, and laid out a course: There were two long stretches, called "straightaways," each five-eighths of a mile (1 km) long, and two short "straightaways," each one-eighth of a mile (.2 km) long. There were four identical turns, each one-quarter mile (.4 km) in length.

The "straightaways" were 50-feet (15.24-m) wide, and the track broadened to 60-feet (18.28-m) midway through each of the turns. The turns were banked at just over 9 degrees.

The first Indianapolis Race was not just one race, but a series of races, of various kinds. Car against car, car against the clock—Barney Oldfield claimed a world's record of 83.2 mph (133.56 kph) for one mile over a closed course—and motorcycle against motorcycle. There was even a balloon "ascension."

Three days of "events" were scheduled, with the major event to be a 300-mile (482.7-km) auto race on August 21, 1909, the final day. Even before that race started, the deterioration of the crushed rock and tar road surface was evident. With seventeen cars pounding the surface in the final race, the track began to disintegrate.

Officials of the American Automobile Association, in charge of the race, stopped it at 235 miles (378.1 km) when it became obvious that the course conditions had become too dangerous.

Above: the very first race at Indianapolis: cars 18 and 19 are Stoddard-Daytons; 30 and 31 are Buicks, entered by David Dunbar Buick himself.
Below: just before the Indianapolis Speedway was paved in 1909. The first surface was a mixture of crushed stone and tar. It didn't prove strong enough for the stresses of racing; it wore out before the first racing session was over.

Fisher and his associates immediately decided they would have to have the best, strongest surface available. After making some tests, they decided on bricks, which would be laid in cement. Certainly, nothing could be stronger than a brick wall, laid flat on the ground. Purchase orders were immediately issued for 3.2 million of the best quality bricks, plus many tons of the best cement.

The bricks of what came to be known as "the brickyard" were in place by December 1909, but subfreezing weather discouraged not only fans, but drivers as well. In the summer of 1910, racing "events" were held on the Memorial Day, Independence Day, and Labor Day weekends, but attendance (which is to say gate receipts) was disappointing, even when prices were cut to encourage attendance.

Fisher got together with auto manufacturers, race drivers, and his partners, and it was decided that rather than having a series of events they would have one event: the biggest in racing. The race would cover 500 miles (804.5 km), a distance that would not only subject cars and drivers to the most grueling punishment, but that would take long enough to justify the stiff price they intended to charge the public.

To attract newspaper interest, the track announced that it would award a first prize of $25,000 to the winners. This was an enormous sum in an era when a worker brought home about ten dollars for a fifty-hour work week.

While there were those who said that all Fisher and his associates were doing was throwing good money after bad (after all, the novelty of automobiling was growing a little old), Fisher stuck to his guns. And despite the prices, the fans flocked to the first Indianapolis 500, on Memorial Day, 1911.

Six hours 42 minutes and 8 seconds after the checkered flag had dropped, Ray Harroun, at the wheel of No. 32, a six-cylinder Marmon "Wasp," crossed the finish line. He had set a dazzling speed of 74.59 mph (120.02 kph). A total of $27,550 was paid out in prize money. Harroun won $10,000. Prize money at Indianapolis has grown over the years. In 1975 the total prize money was $1,001,321.

Above: Ray Harroun at the wheel of No. 32, the Marmon "Wasp" in which he won the first Indianapolis 500. Note the handles on the fuel tank covers behind him; the "vertical stabilizer" on the pointed tail, and the sturdy leather strap holding the hood in place. Below: racing through Turn No. 1 in the first Indianapolis 500, May 30, 1911, are Numbers 8 (Joe Jagersberger) and 9 (Will Jones). Louis Disbrow is at the wheel of a Pope-Hartford (No. 5).

Joe Dawson, driving a four-cylinder National, won the 1912 Indianapolis 500, upping the speed to 78.72 mph (126.66 kph). The next four races, 1913 through 1916, went to European cars. A French Peugeot won in 1913 and in 1916; a French Delage won in 1914, and a Mercedes in 1915. Ralph de Palma, an American, drove the Mercedes.

Below: the start of the 1912 Indianapolis 500, showing the Stutz Pace Car 29. De Palma is at the wheel of the Mercedes, No. 4. Right: Barney Oldfield (at the wheel) couldn't do better than fifth place in the 1914 Indianapolis 500 in his Stutz. That was good enough, however, to make the Stutz Bearcat (a "version" of the race car) the dream of every American male of the period.

Above: Ralph de Palma raises his hand to acknowledge the roar of the crowd as he crosses the finish line to win the 1915 Indianapolis 500. Below: this Mercer ran badly in the 1915 Indianapolis 500. Note the tire tread; the water temperature gauge on the radiator and some of the first "knock-off" wheels. Right: Dario Resta in No. 17, a French Peugeot, takes the checkered flag at the 1916 Indianapolis 500.

Alice Ramsey, the first cross-country woman automobilist, and her crew. Her companions were along for moral support only; she was the only one who knew how to drive.

ALICE RAMSEY: WOMAN DRIVER

Alice Ramsey shocked the world of the automobilists, not to mention some of her New Jersey family and neighbors, when she announced that she intended to be the first woman to drive across the country.

Accompanied by three of her friends, none of whom could drive, she set out in the spring of 1909 from New York to Los Angeles at the wheel of a Maxwell. She surprised practically everybody but her passengers by making it without incident. In 1968, more than half a century later, Alice Ramsey very quietly drove from Los Angeles to New York. No one paid any particular notice to the dignified gentlewoman on that trip.

OTHER RACES AND RACERS

Racing in America was first and foremost a capitalistic under-taking. Even the drivers, who became national heroes, readily admitted they were in it for the money, and the prospects of making money stirred the interests of entrepreneurs all over the country.

Only Vanderbilt, who had money already, didn't really care about it, and it's a matter of record that the Vanderbilt Races lost money. Other races, thousands of them—sometimes in connection with county or state fairs, sometimes races by themselves —were held whenever the promoters decided there was money to be made.

This Locomobile, driven by George Robertson, won the 1908 Vanderbilt Cup Race.

The American Automobile Association (formed March 4, 1902), announced that it was in charge of all auto racing, but was ignored whenever the promoters felt like it. And they felt like it whenever AAA rules threatened to cost money.

Some races were completely honest, held under the best safety conditions, and others were the exact opposite. Manufacturers who felt that a win would help car sales felt that whatever it cost to win—either money spent building a faster car or else money given to the driver of a competitive car not to win— was a perfectly legitimate business expense.

Board tracks had an appeal to promoters. They were inside, and races could be held despite the weather. They were expensive to build, however, and when they burned, the fire was hard to put out. Public officials generally disapproved of them because they were a hazard.

Since there was really no governing body for racing, drivers and manufacturers could call themselves "champions" on sometimes rather flimsy evidence. No one really seemed to mind, which lent support to the cynical statement that people didn't watch racers to see races, but rather to see wrecks.

Indianapolis was honest from the start, of course, and when the AAA was in charge, Daytona Beach was too. The Savannah Challenge Race of 1910 was held in high regard, and so were the Elgin (Illinois) Road Races.

Harold Strane races around the Atlanta, Georgia, Board Track in 1909. The car is a Buick. Note how only a couple of two-by-fours separate the spectators from the track. Drivers were instructed in the case of a blowout, to steer for the center of the track. Most of the time, they could do it.

Paul Gelnon, at the wheel of No. 35, a ''Falcon,''
wears a face mask against the dust as he rolls through
the start/finish line at the 1910 Savannah Challenge.

Above: "The Pits" at the 1910 Savannah Challenge Races.
The cars are Marmons. Joe Dawson is at right. Below: Lee
Bible poses proudly by the side of his enormous White
Triplex on the beach at Daytona. He was later killed driv-
ing this car. Firestone had already learned the publicity
value of having their tires used on racing cars.

Above: seconds after this photo was snapped in the 1911 Elgin Road Races, the right front tire of Dave Buck's Pope-Hartford (No. 3) blew out. The enormous car turned over, killing Buck instantly and fatally injuring his riding mechanic, Steve Jacobs, who died a few hours later. Car No. 1 is an Alco. Below: Louis Chevrolet at the wheel of a Buick in Atlanta in 1913.

THE ELGIN RACES

Chicago, of course, claimed to be the site of the first auto race in America, and the idea of letting Indianapolis steal all the auto racing headlines was too much for proud Chicagoans. The problem was that Indianapolis had a race track, and Chicago didn't. But building a track cost a lot of money: it was cheaper to declare that over-the-road racing was the true test of driver and car. So the Elgin Races were held as Road Races.

THE CHEVROLET BROTHERS
AND ALBERT CHAMPION

By and large, the pay for race drivers in Europe was, and still is, prestige, which caused a number of European drivers to come to the United States to race for wealth.

The names of two of them have entered the language: Chevrolet and Champion. Albert Champion was a French racer and mechanic. He came to the attention of the automotive wheeler-dealer of all time: William Crapo Durant, founder of General Motors. Durant listened carefully to Champion's idea for a new-fangled spark plug, one using a ceramic insulator, and provided the money for him to develop his idea. The result was the AC (for Albert Champion) Company, now the AC Spark Plug Division of General Motors.

Durant's relationship with the Chevrolet brothers, Louis and Arthur, was even more interesting. They were Swiss-born French race drivers. Durant pitted the two against each other in a race.

Arthur lost the race. He had taken no chances. He was immediately hired, at a splendid salary, as personal driver to William Crapo Durant, who liked to be driven fast, but safely. Louis was also put on the payroll, and told to design a car that would bear his last name.

ACROSS THE COUNTRY BY TRUCK

The Alco Company, which had spent a very large amount of money building rather unsuccessful race cars, lost enthusiasm for auto racing but decided, in 1912, that they could still capture the public's eye by driving one of their trucks cross-country.

The truck had hard-rubber tires and a top speed of around 11 mph (17.69 kph). The only modification to it for the trip was the installation of a large searchlight on a swivel. As it reached San Francisco, it became the first cross-country delivery by motor truck.

EDDIE RICKENBACKER

One of the most popular racers of the time was Eddie Rickenbacker. He was admired for his mechanical skill as well as his icy nerves on the tracks.

When the United States entered World War I, and General John J. Pershing sailed from Hoboken, New Jersey, to assume command of the American Expeditionary Force, Rickenbacker suddenly decided he had to go. Through an influential friend, he enlisted the night before Pershing's ship left, and sailed with it as a private driver. (He was not, legend to the contrary, Pershing's personal driver.)

Once he got to France, Rickenbacker decided that he could make a far greater contribution to the American war effort than chauffeuring officers around, and so he talked his way into being sent to flying school, although according to the regulations he was too old and couldn't pass the physical examination. A friendly doctor, who had known him as a race driver, made a "mistake" on the examination report, and Rickenbacker was taught how to fly.

When the war ended, he was Captain Eddie Rickenbacker, America's greatest ace and commanding officer of the "Hat In The Ring Squadron"; he returned wearing the blue-starred ribbon of the Congressional Medal of Honor around his neck.

After the war, he built an unsuccessful automobile, "The Rickenbacker" that was far ahead of its time (it had brakes on all four wheels!) and then turned his attention to aviation. He took over a fledgling airline and built it into Eastern Airlines. During World War II, Rickenbacker's plane was forced to ditch in the Pacific Ocean, and the crew floated around for twenty-four days before being rescued. The others with him, all young enough to be his sons, gave him credit for keeping them alive during their ordeal.

Howard Aitken and Eddie Rickenbacker at the Sheepshead Bay (New York) Raceway in 1916.

THE WAR YEARS

As the war in Europe grew larger, and it became evident that America would be involved, racing slowed to a stop. The last Vanderbilt Race was held in Santa Monica, California, in 1916, and racing was halted at Indianapolis in 1917 and 1918.

However, in 1915 Cannonball Baker raced a Stutz across the North American continent, to set a fresh record that endured for a long time, and Wild Bill Davidson set a gas engine record for the measured mile of 25.2 seconds in a Blitzen-Benz in 1917.

During World War I, the Indianapolis Speedway became an aviation repair depot for America's newborn Army Air Corps. The longer straightaways were used as landing strips for Army aircraft flying between Dayton, Ohio, and Rantoul, Illinois. One hundred acres of the property were planted in hay and grain.

Cannonball Baker, who after World War II was to become the first commissioner of NASCAR (stock car) Racing, set a cross-country record in this Stutz in 1915.

THE POSTWAR YEARS
AT INDIANAPOLIS

Racing resumed in 1919, but it wasn't quite the same as it had been before the war. In a move intended both to encourage the design of more efficient engines and also to keep Speedway racing from becoming a contest to see who could build the largest engine, the rules concerning allowable engine displacement had been changed, starting in 1911. For the first race, in 1911, engines of up to 600 cubic inches (9,832.2 cm^3) were permitted. This was reduced to 450 cubic inches (7,374.15 cm^3) in 1913 and to 300 cubic inches (4,916.1 cm^3) in 1915. (Engine displacement is the volume of the cylinders.)

The Pace Car for the 1919 Indianapolis Race, a V-12 Packard, received the most tumultuous applause ever heard at Indianapolis as it drove around the course carrying the official referee, Captain Eddie Rickenbacker.

The race went to a Peugeot, a four-cylinder monster with a 274.6-cubic inch (4,499.87-cm^3) engine, which covered the 500 miles (804.5 km) in 5 hours, 40 minutes, 42.87 seconds, which translated to 88.05 mph (141.67 kph).

Just about as soon as the race was over, officials announced a further reduction in legal engine size, this time down to 183 cubic inches (2,998.82 cm^3). The 1920 race was won by an American car, a Monroe, with Gaston Chevrolet at the wheel. His engine had a displacement of 182.5 cubic inches (2,990.62 cm^3) but his speed (88.62 mph/142.59 kph) was a fraction of a second *faster* than that of the enormous Peugeot of a year before. Race officials congratulated themselves on having made the right decision.

The next year, 1921, the speed went up exactly one mile per hour (to 89.62 mph/144.2 kph) when Tommy Milton took the race in a Frontenac. The era of special "Indianapolis" cars had begun.

Above: Tommy Milton at the wheel of his Disteel-
Frontenac, winner of the 1921 Indianapolis 500.
Right: the starting lineup of the 1923 Indianapolis 500.
The official Pace Car is a Cole V-8. V-8 engines were the rage,
following the success of the design in World War I aircraft engines.

In 1922 (with Eddie Rickenbacker serving as the starter) a
Murphy Special upped the speed to 99.48 mph (160.06 kph). Then
the officials cut permissible engine size again, this time to 122
cubic inches (1,999.22 cm³). This dropped the winning speed in
1923 to 90.95 mph (146.34 kph), with Tommy Milton at the wheel
of the H.C.S. Special.

A rather distinguished old-time racer was called to serve as
the referee of the 1924 Indianapolis 500, when Eddie Rickenbacker pleaded he was too busy to participate as he was building his own car (for the public, not the track). The old-timer's
name was Henry Ford. A Duesenberg Special, displacing 121.9
cubic inches (1,997.58 cm³), won the race, with an average speed
of 98.23 mph (158.05 kph).

The Pace Car the next year was a Rickenbacker V-8, and in 1925, for the first time, the winner's average speed was over 100 mph (160.9 kph). Peter de Paolo drove a Duesenberg over the 500 miles (804.5 km) in 4 hours, 56 minutes, 39.46 seconds to win.

And just about as soon as that race was over, the track officials announced yet another reduction in engine displacement, this time to 91.5 cubic inches (1,499.41 cm³). The engine designers were ready this time, however, and the winner's speed for 1926 dropped only about 5 mph (8 kph), to 95.904 mph (154.31 kph).

In 1927 the winning speed was up to 97.545 mph (156.95 kph) with the tiny engine, and it rose to 99.482 mph (160.07 kph) in 1928, dropped to 97.585 mph (154.31 kph) in 1929, and finally broke the "century mark" again in 1930, when Billy Arnold drove his Miller-Harz Special to victory with a speed of 100.448 mph (161.62 kph).

Louis Meyer drove this Miller Special (90.2 cubic inches [1,478.1 cm³]; 99.48 mph [160.07 kph]) to win the 1928 Indianapolis 500.

1st Place Winner
Louis Meyer - Miller Special.
Indianapolis Motor Speedway
16th Annual 500 Mile Race 1928.

OTHER RACING

Without much success, race promoters scheduled races whenever they thought they could entice enough paying customers to make a profit. It was a rare state (or for that matter, county) fair that didn't have a "Grand Championship" race of some kind, featuring either Indianapolis type cars or cars that *looked* like Indianapolis cars or were miniatures (called midgets).

But one by one, the auto race tracks—except for Indianapolis—either went broke or were broken up to make room for housing developments. When the Great Depression of 1929 came, it dealt a vicious blow to auto racing as well as everything else.

The beach at Daytona required little maintenance, and racing continued there.

THE RICKENBACKER YEARS
AT INDIANAPOLIS

Eddie Rickenbacker's Rickenbacker automobile was not a commercial success (probably, most people said, because it was too far ahead of its time), and he moved back into racing with his purchase of Indianapolis in 1929. About the first thing he did was authorize the increase of engine displacement.

Rickenbacker had seen that the automobile manufacturers had just about withdrawn from Indianapolis racing, and he knew why they had. There was no incentive for them to stay in. They were in the business of selling cars, and the public was unlikely to rush to buy a new Buick because a Buick *sponsored* car (a highly specialized racing machine, bearing little or no resemblance to Buicks on the showroom floor) had made a 500-mile (804.5-km) left turn at over 100 mph (160.9 kph).

Above: the 1932 winner, a Miller-Hartz Special, Fred Frame at the wheel, averaged 104.14 mph (167.57 kph) for the distance, with a 182.0 cubic-inch (2,982.43 cm³) engine. Note that the water temperature gauge is gone from the top of the radiator. Above right: this is the Pirrung Special, in which Wilbur Shaw, one of the greatest drivers ever, won second place in the 1935 Indianapolis 500. With a 220 cubic-inch (3,605.14 cm³) engine, he averaged 105.99 mph (170.54 kph), losing to Kelly Petillo in a Gilmore Speedway Special. That's a difference of one-quarter of a mile per hour over a 500 mile course. Below right: Shaw at the wheel of his Boyle Special, which he drove at 114.27 mph (183.87 kph) to win the 1940 Indianapolis 500. He had also won the 1937 (113.58 mph [182.75 kph]) and the 1939 (115.03 mph [185.09 kph]) and had come in second in the 1938 (115.58 mph [185.97 kph]).

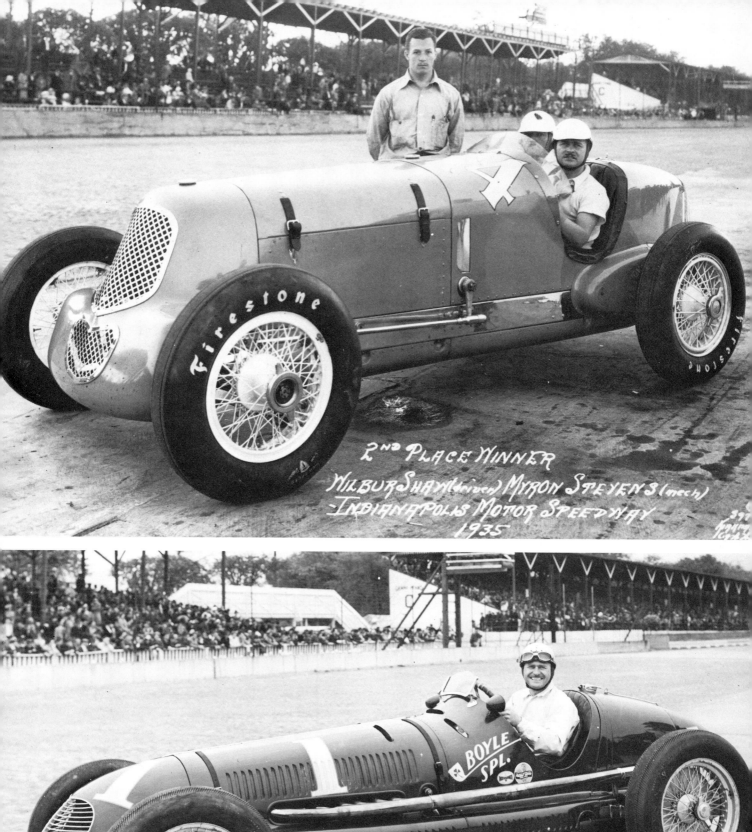

2nd Place Winner
Wilbur Shaw (driver) Myron Stevens (mech)
Indianapolis Motor Speedway
1935

Winner
Wilbur Shaw
Indianapolis Motor Speedway

Rickenbacker banned superchargers, which permitted the manufacturers quite literally to get back in the race. Engines built by Chrysler, Reo, Hupmobile, Hudson, and Buick powered cars that raced against special racing engines until 1938.

None won, although they came close. Studebaker, for example, captured five of the first twelve positions in 1933.

In 1938, an international agreement specified a maximum engine displacement of 183 cubic inches (2,998.82 cm³) for supercharged engines and 274 cubic inches (4,490.04 cm³) for "unblown" power plants. That ended the era of "stock" engines at Indianapolis, and opened another, that of "exotic fuels." Anything that would burn in a cylinder was permitted.

Rickenbacker sold the track to Tony Hulmann, Jr., in 1945.

THE FASTEST CARS IN THE WORLD

On December 18, 1898, the Count de Chasseloup-Laubat drove his Jeantaud electric car over a measured kilometer at Acheres, near Paris, and announced that his blazing 63.21 kph (39.29 mph) established his car as the fastest car in the world, and himself as the fastest driver.

On April 29, 1899, he was back at Acheres to try to up his record, and this time he had competition, Camille Jenatzy, driving an electric car he'd built himself. Jenatzy upped the top speed to 41.42 mph (66.64 kph) over the measured kilometer. Count de Chasseloup-Laubat bettered that with 43.69 mph (70.3 kph). Jenatzy ran again, this time at 49.42 mph (79.51 kph). The Count topped this with 57.60 mph (92.68 kph), and Jenatzy, in the final run, came out as the fastest driver in the world with 65.79 mph (105.86 kph), making him the first man to run officially at more than a mile a minute.

In 1904 Henry Ford (driving a Ford) became the first man to

run a-mile-and-a-half a minute (91.37 mph/147.01 kph) but before the year was over, millionaire sportsman William K. Vanderbilt, Jr., driving a Mercedes, was clocked officially at 92.30 mph (148.51 kph). And before the year was over, Frenchmen L. Rigolly (Gobron-Brillie car; 103.55 mph/166.61 kph) and P. Barras (Darracq car; 104.52 mph/168.17 kph) became the first to exceed 100 mph (160.9 kph) over a measured distance.

The two-miles-a-minute (3.22 kpm) title went to V. Hemery, who drove a Darracq at 125.95 mph (202.65 kph) in 1905. The speed climbed steadily upward over the years until measured-course racing moved to the sands at Daytona. On March 29, 1927, Sir Henry Segrave ran his Sunbeam over the sand at 203.79 mph (327.9 kph), breaking the 200-mph (321.8-kph) barrier.

The 300-mph (482.7-kph) barrier fell at the Bonneville Salt Flats in Utah on September 3, 1935, when Sir Malcolm Campbell set a record of 301.13 mph (484.52 kph) in his Bluebird. (The Bluebird is now on display at the Museum of Speed, Daytona Beach.)

**Sir Malcolm Campbell with his "Bluebird" at Daytona
where he took it to 276.82 mph (445.40 kph) in 1935.**

The 400-mph (643.6-kph) barrier didn't fall for twenty-eight years, and then only to a machine that was deemed technically to be a motorcycle. Craig Breedlove's three-ton jetcar was quite a motorcycle. It was about as big as a jet fighter plane, without wings, and powered by a jet airplane engine. It was disqualified for the fastest car competition because the machine had three wheels, and because it was propelled by jet-thrust, rather than by powered wheels. It ran at 407.45 mph (655.68 kph) over the Bonneville Salt Flats on August 5, 1963. The following year, however, a wheel-driven vehicle—the "Proteus Blue Bird" with Donald Campbell driving—broke the 400-mile barrier at Lake Eyre, Australia. His measured speed was 403.1 mph (648.59 kph).

Craig Breedlove stands beside his "Spirit of America" just before his record-breaking 407.45 mph (655.59 kph) run in 1963. This is the car disqualified from holding the title because it was a "motorcycle."

Art Arfons and his "Green Monster." Arfons drove this car at 576.55 mph (927.67 kph) to take the title as the world's fastest driver, November 7, 1965, only to lose it back to Craig Breedlove eight days later when Breedlove ran through the speed traps at 600.60 mph (966.54 kph) in his "Spirit of America."

In 1965 Art Arfons drove his "Green Monster," powered by another aircraft jet but with driven wheels, at 434.20 mph (698.63 kph) at Bonneville. But this record didn't last long.

Craig Breedlove's Spirit of America upped the top speed to 468.72 mph (754.17 kph). Arfons upped it again to 536.71 mph (863.57 kph), then Breedlove came back with 555.10 mph (893.16 kph) in 1965. And then Arfons was back again the same year with 576.55 mph (927.67 kph).

Gary Gabelich's "The Blue Flame." Powered by a rocket engine burning liquified natural gas and hydrogen peroxide, "The Blue Flame" set the world's speed record of 622.41 mph (1,001.64 kph) on October 23, 1970.

Craig Breedlove ended the year by being the first man to drive at better than 600 mph (600.60 mph/966.37 kph). This record lasted until 1970, when Gary "Gabe" Gabelich entered the competition and drove his car entitled "The Blue Flame" across the salt flats at 622.41 mph (1001.46 kph) on October 23, 1970. His engine generated 16,000 lbs (7,257.44 kg) of thrust while making his two runs over the measured mile at 617.602 mph and 627.287 mph for the 622.41 mph (1001.46 kph) average speed.

GRAND PRIX RACING

The oldest and, outside the United States, the most popular form of racing is Grand Prix, which means "Big Prize" in the language of the French, who drew up the first rules for auto racing in 1906.

There are more than a dozen kinds of Grand Prix racing, each called a "Formula." Formula 1 is the most important and is generally recognized to be the fastest and most dangerous form of racing. Formula 1 racing cars are designed and built solely for the "Grand Prix, Formula 1 Circuit," which includes races all over the world for the world's championship. The American Grand Prix is held at Watkins Glen, New York. The most famous of all Grand Prix Races is the one held on the streets of Monaco.

While the rules for Formula 1 Racing fill a thick book, generally they require that a car weigh no less than 530 kg (just over 1100 lbs), not including a 30-kg (66.14-lb) "safety package" (fire extinguishers, roll bars, and explosion-resistant fuel tanks). The engine capacity is limited to 3,000 cubic centimeters (183 cu in), or 1,500 cm^3 (91.5 cu in) if supercharged. Only regular gasoline is permitted. Formula 1 races must be at least 300 km (186 mi), and no more than 400 km (248 mi), in length.

Formula 2 Grand Prix cars are not quite as fast as Formula 1, and Formula 2 racing serves as sort of a training ground for race drivers. Gearboxes are limited to five forward speeds (Formula 1 cars have as many as ten), and the engines must use a cylinder block of no more than six cylinders from a "production car" of which no less than five hundred were made in a year. Formula 1 cars have no such restrictions. Many Formula 1 cars have twelve-cylinder engines of which no more than half a dozen have ever been built.

Formula 3 and Formula 4 racing restricts even further the size, weight, and engine size of racing cars. Many amateurs race in these categories. Other categories include Formula Ford (which requires use of the 1,600 cc [97.6 cu in] Ford engine); Formula 5000 (mass produced V-8 engines of no more than 5,000 cm³ [305 cu in] displacement—in other words standard American passenger car engines); Formula V (the Volkswagen engine), and many others.

Left: a Formula 1 racing car, this one built by John Player and entered in the United States Grand Prix at Watkins Glen, New York. Note the size of the rear tires. Directly above the driver's head is an airscoop to feed air to the carburetor system. Behind the scoop is an airfoil, sort of a wing designed to give the car greater stability. Above: the Players 200 International race in Toronto, Canada. The Canadian Grand Prix, with world class Formula 1 cars, began in 1966.

Above: the driver of this Formula 1 car, which ran at Watkins Glen, was Lella Lombardi, an Italian woman who came to be known as "The Tigress of Turin." Below: the start of the Grand Prix de France race at the Charade Track, Clermont-Ferrand. These are all Formula 1 cars. Right: Formula 2 cars line up at Brand's Hatch, England, for the start of the Rothamn's International Race.

LE MANS

"Le Vingt-Quarte Heures de Le Mans" (The 24 Hours of LeMans) has been described as the toughest race of all. The race is against time (twenty-four hours of it), round the clock, through rain and fog, in cars driven by teams of drivers, around one of the oldest race courses in existence, at Le Mans, France.

The American version of this race is held at Sebring, Florida, every year.

The start of the Fiftieth Anniversary
24 Hours of Le Mans, June 9, 1973.

MONZA

Monza is a race against distance, as well as against other cars. It is held annually at Monza, Italy, for a distance of 1,000 km (620 mi).

Mario Andretti, who won at Indianapolis and at Daytona, has also brought home victories from Europe. Here he is taking the checkered flag at the Monza 1,000 kilometer race, April 25, 1974. He drove 1,003.98 km (623.77 mi) in 4 hours 45 minutes, 57.4 seconds, to win at an average speed of 210.65 kph (130.60 mph).

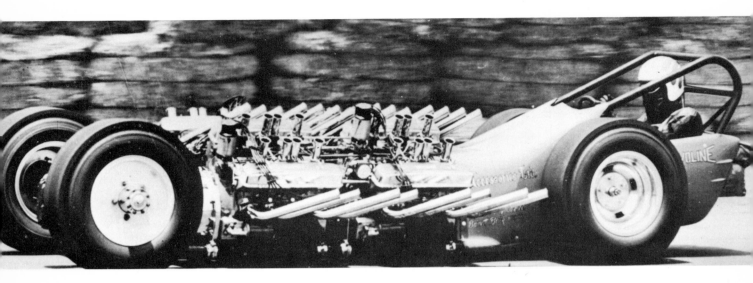

Above: actor Tommy Ivo installed four Buick V-8 engines in his dragster, with each engine driving one wheel. Below: one of the most rugged of the off the road races in the Mint 400, held at Las Vegas, Nevada. The race is four laps around a 90-mile (144.81-km) course through the desert. Gene Hirst took 9 hours, 31.46 minutes to complete the race in first place. The prize was seven thousand dollars, much less than the car cost.

DRAG RACING

Drag racing is a race of acceleration. Cars line up, two at a time, side by side, and when signaled by a light, race from a standing start down a course only one-quarter mile in length. There are virtually no limits on engine size, or kind of fuel, although strict safety standards are enforced.

OFF THE ROAD RACING

Off the road racing began with dune buggies and evolved into a form of racing using cars designed for both ruggedness and speed. A relatively small facet of auto racing, it is growing in popularity in the western United States and in Mexico and Africa.

WRINKLE-FENDER

As mentioned earlier, it has been suggested that the real reason some people go to auto races is not to see someone win, but to see someone wreck. Promoters of races have thought this for a long time, and all sorts of "racing" events are held in which the real (if unofficial) purpose is to give the spectators one crash after another.

The most "respectable" of this kind of racing is the "Jalopy Race." These are cars rescued from the junkyard and modified by welding in braces around the radiator, doors, and elsewhere.

Sometimes the "jalopy races" aren't pure
fun. In this race, near Pasadena, California,
the driver was thrown from the car.

Instead of trying to pass another car on the course by going
around it, Jalopy Race technique calls for running into the car
ahead and trying to knock it off the track.

The most honest, if (to racing purists) not entirely the most
respectable of the wrinkle-fender classes, is the demolition derby.
Generally speaking, demolition derby cars are large (the bigger
the better) sedans of the luxury class, and they are completely
unmodified. The winner of a demolition derby is the last car able
to move. The drivers try to run into other cars to disable them.
Head-on collisions are usually (for safety reasons) against the
rules, and the best technique seems to be that of backing into
the other cars.

STOCK CAR RACING

In 1933 Henry Ford put the first Ford V-8 engine on the market. Some people think this gave birth to stock car racing. Others feel that it was inevitable, considering the American hunger to both tinker with engines and compete. And still others feel that stock car racing got its start with moonshine liquor. This argument is supported by the fact that some of the great NASCAR (National Association of Stock Car Auto Racing) drivers unashamedly admit they had begun to race when getting away from alcohol tax agents.

Stock car racing can be extremely dangerous. After this accident in 1973, both drivers retired.

In any event, stock car racing has always been closely tied to Daytona Beach. While Daytona had been the site of professional speedsters all through the postwar years, it had also attracted the amateurs and semiprofessionals.

"Chief among equals" of the semiprofessionals was to be William H. G. France, who had come to Daytona Beach in 1934 with a wife, a baby, and twenty dollars in cash. In the beach and in auto racing involving ordinary people, he saw a whole new world of racing.

Above left: the Beach Course at Daytona in 1935. Cars raced down the beach, made a turn through the dunes onto a parallel road, raced down the road, and then turned back through the dunes onto the beach. Below left: this 1934 Ford didn't make the turn from the beach through the dunes. Below: another early stock car race. These 1933 Ford V-8's are lined up at the Elgin (Illinois) Road Course.

In 1936, the city fathers sponsored a race "over the beach" at Daytona. The race was for "stock cars" rather than racers. They were regular passenger automobiles, and all anyone needed to enter the race was the fee and a willingness to risk his car.

Bill France, who owned a gas station, risked his 1935 Ford in the race. He finished fifth. The 1937 race on the Daytona Beach was promoted by Bill France, who admits he made "a little money." He made "a little more money" the next year, and the year after that, but then his plans to really start promoting races were interrupted by World War II.

In 1946 Bill France was back home and again promoting stock car races over the sand-and-road course at Daytona Beach. And the next year he convened a meeting of race promoters from all over the country at the Ebony Bar (now LeRoy Jenkins's "Palace Inn") in Daytona. France proposed the formation of an organization to control stock car racing, most importantly to make it honest and safe. With the exception of Indianapolis, and a very few other places, auto racing had deteriorated in quality. Promoters of something less than sterling honesty were running races that did not necessarily go to the swiftest racers.

France proposed to change all this. Despite a good deal of scoffing and some outright hostility aimed against him, he proceeded to do just that.

The new organization was named the National Association For Stock Car Automobile Racing, and Bill France was its first president. He remained president until a new one was elected in 1972: William H. G. France, Jr., otherwise known as "Bill Junior."

The first thing NASCAR did was issue a rule book for the 1948 season. All four rules fit on a medium-sized sheet of paper that could be folded to the size of a business envelope. Over the years, the book has been expanded to over a hundred pages.

Left: a 1936 Ford takes the checkered flag on the beach at Daytona in 1938.

Above: the organizational meeting of NASCAR. This is where stock car racing as it is known today was born. Big Bill France is at the right of the head of the table. Right: the NASCAR Beach Course in 1949. The starting pack is at the upper end of the road portion of the course. Spectator cars line the infield on the beach.

When the word spread that NASCAR was what it said it was, an organization not only to promote stock car racing, but to guarantee to both spectators and drivers that everything promised would be delivered, the sport burst into life. Drivers who had been reluctant to compete for prize money that often never was paid now drove long distances to compete, and tried hard. And the fans came . . . and paid . . . to see them.

And as important, the auto manufacturers came back into racing, for exactly the same reasons they had been in racing a half-century before: to sell cars to people who thought racing a car was the best possible way to tell how good it was.

Tracks for NASCAR stock car racing sprang up all over the South as fan interest in the sport grew. And then Bill France had another wild idea. He would build at Daytona a super-speedway, a track that would handle the fastest stock cars, no matter how much they were souped up.

There was room for only one speedway, skeptics argued, and there was one already, at Indianapolis. Besides, common ordinary cars wouldn't stand up to the stress of a 500-mile (804.5-km) race. Everybody knew that.

Above: NASCAR races on Daytona Beach in 1955. The Pure Oil Company provided gasoline free for the publicity value. Right: by 1955, fans were lined up all around the course, not just at the start/finish lines and turns. Here a Buick leads an Oldsmobile into the turn from the road to the beach.

Above: the pits at the 1955 Beach races at Daytona. These cars are lined up to try for the Century Club. Anyone could enter. Drivers pumped their tires to 70 lbs (31.8 kg) of pressure and took a shot through a timed, measured mile. Those that did it in 100 mph (160.9 kph) or better got a certificate stating they were members of the Century Club. Above left: the driver of Ford No. 12 in the 1955 race was Ralph Moody. He gave up driving to become a builder of engines and race cars. Holman-Moody engines became famous to stock car fans. Below left: by 1956, manufacturer participation had become enormous. Here Joe Weatherly, a NASCAR racing great, drives a Ford Motor Company sponsored Ford.

France built his track.

The first Daytona 500-mile race was held on February 22, 1959, on the just completed course. Truth to tell, the racing professionals at Indianapolis looked down their noses at the "amateurs" of NASCAR until the race results were in. The 1959 Indianapolis winner, driving a car designed for nothing but 500 miles of high-speed driving, a Leader Car 500, had taken Indianapolis with an average speed of 135.857 mph (218.59 kph). "Amateur" Lee Petty, driving a 1959 Oldsmobile, No. 42, won the first Daytona 500-mile race with an average speed of 135.521 mph (218.05 kph)—three-tenths of a mile an hour slower over the same distance.

There were those who sniffed, too, at what happened after the race. Petty's son Richard, not quite old enough to drive legally, jumped in the winning car and drove it off.

They were to see more of Richard Petty in the winner's circle. Five years later he was back, this time driving himself. His father had used racing number 42, so Richard politely followed him, with No. 43. In 1964, Richard Petty took the Daytona 500 in Plymouth No. 64, with a speed of 154.334 mph (248.32 kph). A. J. Foyt won Indianapolis that year with a speed of 147.350 mph (237.09 kph). Petty came back to win the Daytona 500 again in 1966 in another Plymouth and a speed of 160.627 mph (258.45 kph).

(Clockwise, from upper left) Daytona Before: Volusia Boulevard, outside Daytona Beach, Florida, where Bill France built the Daytona International Speedway. Note the small dirt track in left center. Daytona During Construction: Bill France banked the turns at Daytona so steeply that special construction was necessary to pave them. Cars must go about 70 mph (112.63 kph) to keep from slipping sideward. Daytona Afterward: The track on opening day, 1959. The small track is still visible. The large area in the center of the track is a lake, from which sand was dug to build the track. The first fans sat on these bleachers. Now stands capable of holding nearly a hundred thousand spectators ring the track. This is the start/finish straightaway on opening day.

Lee Petty (Car No. 42) leads the pack through the North Turn in the first Daytona 500, February 22, 1959.

A young Italian-American from Nazareth, Pennsylvania, named Mario Andretti won the 1967 Daytona 500. Two years later the last wise remark was heard about stock car drivers being nothing more than crude amateurs. The winner of the 1969 Indianapolis 500 was a young Italian-American stock car driver named Mario Andretti. Andretti took Indianapolis with a speed of 156.867 mph (252.4 kph). LeeRoy Yarborough won the Daytona 500 that year with 157.950 mph (254.14 kph).

Richard Petty took the 1971 Daytona, and the next year, A. J. Foyt moved from Indianapolis to Daytona to win the 1972 Daytona 500. Petty, the first stock car racer ever to earn more than a million dollars in prize money, returned to Daytona in 1973 and 1974. He has won more races there than anyone else.

A. J. FOYT

BENNY PARSONS

BOBBY UNSER

MARIO ANDRETTI

RICHARD PETTY

LEEROY YARBOROUGH

LEE PETTY

Right: they're off and running!
The start of the 1975 Indianapolis
500. Above: this spectacular crash
occurred on the 127th lap of the 1975
Indianapolis 500. The driver survived.

Indianapolis has remained the most famous American race of all, of course, and it grows bigger and faster every year. But so does NASCAR. There are now six NASCAR super-speedways, and auto racing, which has become the most popular of all spectator sports, shows every sign of keeping that distinction.

BIBLIOGRAPHY

Butterworth, William. **Wheels and Pistons.** New York: Four Winds Press, 1971.

——. **The High Wind.** New York: Grosset & Dunlap, 1971.

Donovan, Frank R. **Wheels for a Nation.** New York: Thomas Y. Crowell, 1965.

Flink, James J. **America Adopts the Automobile, 1895–1910.** Boston: M.I.T. Press, 1970.

Hough, Richard, and Frostick, M. **A History of the World's Sports Cars.** New York: Harper & Row, Publishers, Inc., 1965.

Lurani, Giovanni. **History of the Racing Car.** New York: Thomas Y. Crowell, 1972.

Purdy, Ken. **Ken Purdy's Book of Automobiles.** New York: Playboy Press, 1972.

Ross, Frank, Jr. **Racing Cars and Great Races.** New York: Lothrop, Lee & Shepard, 1972.

Stein, Ralph. **The American Automobile.** New York: Random House, 1971.

INDEX